Never Be
Old Enough
To Know Better

and You Will Succeed
in Life and Business

by
Samuel K. Freshman

This publication is designed to provide accurate and authoritative information in regard to subject matter covered. It is sold and distributed with the understanding that the author and publisher are not engaged in rendering legal, accounting, or other professional services. If legal advice or other expert assistance is required, the services of a competent professional person should be sought.

No part of this book may be reproduced, stored in a retrieval system, or transmitted in any form, or by any means, graphic, electronic, mechanical, photocopying, recording, taping, or otherwise, without prior written express consent from the publisher. The exception is brief quotations embodied in critical articles or reviews, which give full credit and reference to this book.

Never Be
Old Enough
To Know Better

and You Will Succeed
in Life and Business

by
Samuel K. Freshman

DEDICATION

I would like to dedicate this book to my wife, Ardyth, my grandfather William Krelitz, my parents Earl and Leona Freshman, and my high school social sciences teacher Miss Hakkinen. They and so many others nurtured my desire for self-improvement and instilled in me courage to try to succeed. They helped me find the self confidence that I could accomplish whatever I set out to do.

I also dedicate this little book to all those who have a desire for more success in their life and business. May it nurture their self-confidence and fuel their commitment to be all that they can be.

ACKNOWLEDGMENTS

I have assembled much of the success principles in this book through personal and professional experience. Therefore, I do not recall exactly where nor from whom much of it originated, but I gratefully acknowledge the many individuals and authors whose words and wisdom helped shape and guide my life. Their influence began in my childhood with my family and grade school teachers and extends today to my grandchildren, who inspired my favorite recommendation, "Why an Adult Should Eat at the Children's Table During Holiday Dinners."

I also owe special thanks to my editor Heidi Clingen, who helped produce this book and encouraged me to create it.

Reviews of
Never Be Old Enough To Know Better

"Sam, I have read your pamphlet from cover to cover and plan to keep it for many years to come. I have cut out a few of the pages in the pamphlet that most spoke to me, and pinned them on the wall of my office where everyone can read them. I couldn't agree more with your statements and advice, and found it so reaffirming to see that a successful person with more years of experience then me has adhered to the same tenets, with excellent results."

—Jennifer Burnham-Grubbs

"Many great points!"

—Robert Pliska, CRE, CPA,
Owner, SVN Property Investment Advisors

"Your tireless effort to help others is demonstrated well over and over ... not only talking about making money, but with a reminder how to deal with life. To me, it's comparable with the Proverbs in the Bible."

—Patrick Hsu, President, Hsu Real Estate
Management & Development

"Your book brings together common sense advice applicable to everyday experiences. It combines reminders pertaining to good planning with ethical guidelines, financial advice with an optimistic outlook. The examples you provide of your personal experiences are particularly helpful to illustrate using the advice."

—A.C. Schwethelm, former chairman of
The Counselors of Real Estate

TABLE OF CONTENTS

SECTION ONE
Principles Of Success In Life

SECTION TWO
Principles Of Success In Business

INTRODUCTION

You may have been scolded as a child, "You are old enough to know better than to do that!" I have wondered, "Are we ever really 'old enough'? At what age are we 'old enough'?" Consider the fact that young people often naturally act with more wisdom than we do—until they learn their bad habits from us!

The older I get, the more I learn how much I don't know. I consider myself to be a "lifelong learner." I have always enjoyed learning from experts on any topic. It keeps you humble, and it's one of the secrets to an active mind and a happy life.

My other books are about specific topics. This book is a collection of what I have learned about success so far! It is a compilation of advice, ideas, and stories that I have written and collected as a lawyer, business owner, and mentor. I realized that many of the lessons I have learned over the years I had often forgotten to apply. That is why I suggest reviewing this book from time to time when you encounter new stages and challenges in your life.

Strive for balance in your personal life and your work life. I have been blessed to have a fulfilling and adventuresome life. I wish the same for you. Mistakes are a fact of life and learning, so do not be afraid of mistakes. This book will help you avoid some of them! May you be fearless and never "old enough to know better." The learning journey never ends.

—Sam Freshman

I WILL NEVER BE TOO OLD TO...

Enjoy a sunset.

Say please and thank you.

Ask for what I want.

Tell a good joke.

Look for opportunities to compliment others.

Take care of my health.

Appreciate the beautiful things in life.

Express gratitude for each day.

Be curious about everyone and everything.

Enjoy nature and the scent of fresh rainfall.

Relax when I listen to classical music.

Tell those who are close to me how much I
appreciate them.

Care about what is happening in the world.

SECTION ONE

Principles Of Success In Life

10 THINGS MY FATHER TAUGHT ME ABOUT LIFE

1. Your family is your first priority.

2. There is a lot of pleasure in helping friends and family succeed.

3. Don't waste money on show. Don't show off.

4. Be polite.

5. Most of what we worry about never happens.

6. Don't worry about what other people think of you. They are too busy worrying about what you think of them.

7. Be there for those who are there for you. Drop those who are only for themselves.

8. It's not the problem; it's how you respond to it.

9. Don't be afraid of anyone. Everyone puts their pants on one leg at a time, just like you do.

10. Always be positive.

WHY ADULTS SHOULD EAT AT THE CHILDREN'S TABLE AT HOLIDAY DINNERS

(Written Sept. 26, 2005)

1. You do not have to wear a tie.

2. You will not be embarrassed if food gets on your clothes or your chin.

3. Your host will not be insulted if you leave something on your plate.

4. You can eat as fast or as slow as you want.

5. You can put your elbows on the table.

6. You can eat with your fingers.

7. You can ask for seconds or thirds.

8. You can put your napkin anywhere.

9. You can make funny faces.

10. You can understand the jokes.

11. You will make new friends.

12. You will be with people you like.

13. You will learn how to have fun.

14. You will feel younger.

15. You will not be asked how your business is going or how you are feeling.

16. You will receive genuine compliments and helpful suggestions.

17. You will not have to talk about the economy or politics.

18. You will not have to listen to gossip.

19. You will not be told what is wrong with kids these days.

20. The conversation will be more entertaining, interesting, and sincere.

My grandfather William Krelitz gave me many wise tips on investments along with spending "quality time" with me. His mentorship included the admonition to remember that "no one can always buy at the bottom and sell at the top" has served me well. He came to America through Ellis Island from Lithuania around 1900. In his pocket was one dollar. He kept that dollar his entire life. Finally, he gave that dollar to me, his first grandson.

15 REASONS WHY AN ADULT SHOULD LISTEN TO CHILDREN

1. You will learn what they think of you.

2. You will learn what they think of themselves.

3. You will learn what is important to them.

4. You will learn what they like and what they dislike.

5. You don't have to talk politics.

6. You will get practical advice.

7. You will have opportunity to express your opinion without interruptions.

8. You will get a fresh approach to problems.

9. You will not be bored.

10. You will become friends.

11. You will gain their appreciation for spending quality time with them.

12. They will remember these conversations when they are older.

13. You will get honest answers.

14. You will be surprised at the answers you get.

15. You can give them what they want and need, rather than what you think they should have.

15 REASONS WHY YOU SHOULD PLAY GAMES WITH CHILDREN

1. They don't cheat.

2. If they do cheat, you won't know.

3. They follow the rules, or make up fun, new rules.

4. They smile and laugh while playing.

5. Your enjoyable challenge is to keep them interested.

6. They play for fun, they don't swear, and they aren't mean.

7. You will be forced to play nice and be on good behavior.

8. You can learn how they think.

9. You can learn their observations about others, which are often more accurate than yours.

10. You can model good habits and share wisdom, which they otherwise might not be receptive to.

11. They have nice friends that you can meet during the game.

12. They appreciate you and will have good memories of you.

13. You can share their excitement and pleasure when they win.

14. They keep the conversation going. You can sit back and listen.

15. They are more interesting to be with now than they will be when they are adults.

10 RULES TO LIVE BY

1. Self-confidence; never arrogance. Admit your mistakes.

2. Life is a process, not an objective. It is a journey, not a destination.

3. Know what your role and goal is in each situation.

4. Have balance in your life.

5. Constantly plan. Plan your day, week, year and life.

6. Change continues taking place at an increasing rate.

7. Challenges are opportunities. Setbacks build character.

8. Have at least one friend each who has one of the following: a boat, vacation home, season tickets, and a golf membership. You don't need to own those yourself.

9. Good parenting is making sure that every child feels they are a special person and are loved and cherished every day. If you are going to have a favorite among your children or family, make sure that everyone feels they are the favorite.

10. Don't live your life without experiencing it. No one ever said on their death bed, "I wish I had spent more time at the office."

TIME DOES MATTER

1. A **century** matters. Ask a historian.

2. A **decade** matters. Ask a medical school graduate.

3. A **year** matters. Ask a child waiting to start kindergarten.

4. A **quarter** matters. Ask a company that missed earnings projections.

5. A **month** matters. Ask the mother whose baby was born early.

6. A **week** matters. Ask a student who didn't study enough to pass.

7. A **day** matters. Ask a candidate awaiting election results.

8. An **hour** matters. Ask someone sitting in a doctor's lobby.

9. A **minute** matters. Ask someone who missed their plane.

10. A **second** matters. Ask a driver who just ran a red light.

11. A **millisecond** matters. Ask a sprinter who won a silver medal.

Some 60 or so years ago, the dorms at Stanford University were considerably less luxurious than now. My first year was spent in a single room with four bunk beds and four desks occupied by myself and my roommates Robert Dalton, Steve Cook, and Noel DeNevers. My mother wanted to know how I was doing, so I had this photo taken with an exceptionally messy desk to prove to her that I still had my sense of humor. While there are many things that I learned (mostly outside of class) during my undergraduate and graduate days at "The Farm," I am still struggling under piles of paper to clear my desk.

WORDS FOR DEALING WITH OTHERS

The Ten Most Important Words:
"We can do this, but we'll have to work together."

The Nine Most Important Words:
"That's a great suggestion and I will consider it."

The Eight Most Important Words:
"How did I ever manage without your help?"

The Seven Most Important Words:
"You were right, and I was wrong."

The Six Most Important Words:
"I'm sorry, it was my fault."

The Five Most Important Words:
"You did a great job."

The Four Most Important Words:
"What do you think?"

The Three Most Important Words:
"Will you please?"

The Two Most Important Words:
"Thank you!"

The Most Important Word:
"We"

The Least Important Word:
"Me"

10 SELF-SABOTAGING BEHAVIORS

1. Pride.

2. Anger.

3. Choosing position over power.

4. Burning bridges.

5. Negative commentary about others.

6. Gratification versus security.

7. Defensiveness.

8. Obsessiveness or compulsiveness.

9. Unrealistic expectations.

10. Attempting to change the direction of a very determined horse.

*I learned several life lessons as a horseman at the Malibu Riding &
Tennis Club. Sometimes you have to accept the fact that the horse
knows better than you.*

MY DEFINITION
OF PERSONAL SUCCESS

1. Not what you make, but what you keep.

2. Not what you say, but what you do.

3. Not how much you eat, but what you eat.

4. Not what you say, but how you say it.

5. Not how many people you may know, but who you know.

6. Not how hard you work, but how smart you work.

7. Not what you take, but what you give.

8. Not what you sell, but what your customer wants.

9. Not what you want, but what you need.

10. Not how much time you have, but how you spend it.

10 TIPS FOR EFFECTIVENESS AND EFFICIENCY

1. Effectiveness is doing the right things. Efficiency is doing things right. When you have a choice, choose effectiveness.

2. It is more important to do the right thing than to do things right. Usually, if the choice is between the important versus the urgent, take care of the urgent first, but only if it also is truly important. If it really needs to be done, do it as efficiently as possible. Do not, however, let the unimportant and urgent distract you from the truly important.

3. You become more effective when you proactively foresee and prevent urgent emergencies and eliminate them as much as possible. Sometimes the urgent will become the important if it is not given immediate attention. Something that appears unimportant can become urgent if not immediately attended to, such as caring for your health.

4. Important *versus* Urgent: Choose Important. Needs *versus* Wants: Choose Needs.

5. Invest *versus* Speculate: Choose Invest.

6. Save *versus* Spend: Choose Save.

7. Simple *versus* Complex: Choose Simple.

8. Listening *versus* Talking: Choose Listening.

9. Analysis *versus* Anger: Choose Analysis.

10. Ask First *versus* Act First. Choose Ask First.

Remember...

It's not your income that makes you rich,
   it's your savings habits.

It's not what your money makes of you,
   it's what you make of your money.

It's not how much you own,
   it's how little you owe.

It's not the "have-to"s or "want-to"s,
   it's the "need-to"s.

It's not what you do,
   it's how you do it.

It's not your habits that control you,
   it's you who controls your habits.

It's not the wishing,
   it's the doing.

It's not the credit card that is the master,
   you are the master.

It's not what you start with,
   it's what you end with.

It's not what you spend together,
   it's how you spend together.

It's not how much you spend for your children,
   it's how much you care for your children.

It's not how much you spend on a gift,
    it's what you give and how you give it.

It's not what you own,
    it's who you are.

It's not what you drive,
    it's what you give up for what you drive.

It's not your wealth,
    it's your health.

It's not how much you spend for fun,
    it's how much fun you have.

It's not what you buy,
    it's how you shop.

It's not where you shop,
    it's what you get.

It's not what you wear,
    it's what you pay for what you wear.

It's not what you know,
    it's what you don't know.

It's not if you owe,
    it's how much you owe.

It's not alligators,
    it's cows that create wealth.

PHRASES TO WATCH OUT FOR

Oxymorons
 1. Cheap date
 2. Bank trust
 3. Honest car dealer
 4. User-friendly software
 5. Government help
 6. Loyal attorney
 7. Brilliant child
 8. Clear instructions
 9. Shortcut
10. Problem-free
11. Satisfaction guaranteed
12. Bargain sale
13. Prompt refund
14. Fat-free
15. Lowest price
16. Best quality
17. Spare time
18. Military intelligence
19. Informed sources
20. Easy assembly
21. Healthy anything
22. Quick profit
23. Handyman
24. Free ride

25. Risk free
26. Turn-key
27. Technical support
28. No sweat

Questionable veracity

29. To tell you the truth...
30. The only solution is...
31. I'm not supposed to tell you, but...
32. Don't tell anyone, but...
33. It hasn't been announced yet, but...
34. I just can't...
35. I absolutely have to...
36. People are saying...
37. I've read that...
38. We assume that...
39. We project that...
40. Our estimations are...
41. That's my bottom line.
42. This is the last chance.
43. It's the only way.
44. This is just between you and me.
45. Take it or leave it.
46. Lots of others are interested.
47. Do you want the truth?
48. Let me tell you honestly.
49. Frankly, I was surprised, too.
50. It's a secret.

Shaky Reassurance

51. It sounds too good to be true, but…
52. With all due respect…
53. I hate to say it, but…
54. Everybody does it this way.
55. Everybody knows.
56. Don't worry; no one knows.
57. It's only boiler plate.
58. It's not important.
59. Don't worry about it!
60. I'll take care of it.
61. You can count on me.
62. Trust me.
63. It's good for you.
64. I will not be late.
65. You won't be sorry.
66. You'll hardly notice.
67. We've always done it like this.
68. This is for your own good.
69. Better late than never.
70. You just never know.
71. It's hard to predict.
72. We've got plenty of time.
73. I'll put a rush on it.
74. I know what I'm doing.
75. It's easy! I do this all day long!

SAM'S PRINCIPLES OF FINANCIAL INDEPENDENCE

1. Daily choices add up.

2. Small savings over a long time create more wealth than big risks.

3. Pay yourself first.

4. Separate wants from needs. Concentrate on needs.

5. Toxic debt is poison.

6. Credit is for emergencies. Pay cash until you reach your goal.

7. Windfalls are capital, not income. Capital is for wealth investment.

8. Never take a risk or purchase an item you cannot afford.

9. Put your own oxygen mask on first.

10. Thoughtful, inexpensive gifts can show you care. Expensive gifts give a false impression and are motivated by insecurity.

11. Enjoyment of luxury is brief. But the anxiety of debt lasts.

12. Get fulfillment from personal relationships, not material things.

13. Why are you shopping? Know the reasons.

14. Resist the urge to indulge in instant gratification; invest instead.

15. Comparison shop first.

16. Buy wholesale whenever possible.

17. Do not make buying decisions based only on labels. Buy value.

18. Buy pre-owned whenever appropriate.

19. Keep price tags and receipts.

20. Keep your funds invested and working for you, but cautiously.

21. Income $1.00; Spend 99¢ = Happiness; Spend $1.01 = Misery.

22. Buy what pays you, not what decreases in value or costs to own.

23. Immediately set aside for taxes.

24. Personal purchases cost 60% more because they are after tax.

25. It's not how much you make, IT'S HOW MUCH YOU KEEP.

26. Don't buy a new or replacement item until you've paid for the last one. Paying for two items at the same time sets you back.

27. Never rely on promises, windfalls, or inheritances. Your lifestyle should be based on your actual, re-curring income.

28. A transaction is not complete until the money is in your bank account. What can go wrong often will.

29. If you are expecting to receive extra money, plan and don't waste it. Apply it toward lasting value: debt reduction and investments.

30. Don't be "penny wise and pound foolish." For example, don't drive a longer distance to save money when the gas or time represents a higher cost.

25 WAYS TO SAVE MONEY

1. Time is money. Everyone needs balance in their life. Plan your time to monetize it so that you're either improving your financial situation, moving yourself towards your financial goals, improving your skills and education, or improving your personal relationships.

2. Your most important resource is your health. Pay attention to it and give it priority. Remember the old adage, "An ounce of prevention is worth a pound of cure."

3. Understand your addictions and weaknesses. Admit them to yourself, get help where you need it, and develop plans and techniques to avoid them.

4. Visualize your goals. Be sure they are achievable, objective, and measurable. Think about your savings habits constantly.

5. Accomplish at least one act every day that carries you toward your goals. The safe and sure way to financial independence is to get there one step at a time, but every day.

6. Learn to think in alternatives. Is there something you can do that will be satisfactory for your goal, but will cost much less than what you were planning to spend?

7. Learn to shop on sale days and at clearance sales. Almost every retailer has periodic sales. Find out when your favorite stores have sales.

8. Be familiar with all the pre-owned merchandise stores in your area. Learn what each has to offer and how often the merchandise changes.

9. Become familiar with bartering. Offer to exchange your services or surplus goods for those goods or services you need.

10. Use generic and "house" or store brands wherever there are major savings. Try generic and house brands of drugs, cosmetics, and many grocery items. Check labels and ingredients to compare.

11. Buy amounts appropriate for your use. If you use a lot of something, the largest size you can afford may give you great savings. If it is something you use very seldom, a smaller size is probably a better investment. If you use a lot, stock up; otherwise don't.

12. Determine when to buy and when to rent. Consider buying anything you intend to keep and use often. For example, the cost of used furniture is often not much more than a few months' rent on new furniture. If you're using something on only a few occasions, borrow it (preferable) or rent it. There is no reason to keep capital tied up in things you do not use.

13. Maximize your living arrangement. Sharing a home or apartment can result in great savings on your single biggest expense.

14. Maximize your ride. Do you and your partner both need a car, or can one of you rideshare to work? This is often the next biggest expense besides a home. Some couples can manage with one car if they live near public transportation or can arrange to ride-share. In some cases, people in metropolitan areas do not need to own a car at all.

15. "Act as if." Incorporate your new behaviors in your life naturally. Think of the old adage, "Fake it till you make it." Act as if your saving habits are already a regular part of your life. Soon they will be.

16. Find an excellent role model. Imitate him or her. Ask your friends who are successful what their savings habits are and how they save.

17. Maximize your associations. Associate with people who are successful savers and investors. Avoid people who tend to encourage you to break your saving habits or who criticize your new savings plans. Remember the phrase, "Birds of a feather flock together." Attract the people who will help, not harm you.

18. Attitude is more important than aptitude. A positive attitude will get you farther in life than all the training in the world. You know how to save. But you will not save until you want to. So have a positive attitude about saving, get started, and learn as you go!

19. Maximize your income. You get more money by making more money or by spending less. It's easier to spend less than to make more.

20. Play free games where you can win things. Fast food outlets and others often run contests and games, and while the odds are against winning a large prize, there may be many smaller prizes that are easy to win.

21. If you are a renter, rent by the month, not by the week. The difference in your total outlay may be dramatic. If the savings are worth it, make the sacrifices necessary to get the deposit together for a monthly lease. If you can lease for twelve months, sometimes landlords will give you a month or two rent-free.

22. Double-up wherever you can. You may not need both a land-line and a cell phone, as many find only a cell phone is more than adequate.

23. Never quit your present job until you have a replacement. It is much easier to get hired if you are

employed when you apply. Gaps in employment are looked on with disfavor by employers.

24. With respect to major items, such as refrigerators and furniture, compare the cost of repair and renovation. Maybe you can put something in "like new" condition for less than the replacement cost.

25. Understand what is wrong with credit cards. If you don't control your use of them, they encourage you to buy things you do not need, with money you do not have, to impress people you should not be trying to impress.

PERSONAL STORIES ABOUT LIFE

1. <u>My First Car Story:</u> I bought my first car with cash. In 1950, after my first year at Stanford University, I took a job that summer as the director of a children's overnight camp in northern Canada. Two of the camp counselors and I decided we wanted to go to the nearest town on our days off to take a break. But we needed a car. Fortunately, we found one, a 1936 Dodge Sedan, for $150, so we each pitched in $50 and bought it. It was no surprise that the car's brakes soon wore out. But we couldn't afford new brakes. Instead, we discovered that we could stop the car by putting it into second gear and coasting to a stop. To our mothers' relief, at the end of the summer, we left the car at the camp. *Remember, the good old days can give you a sense of perspective when you realize you spend more on one tank of gas than you spent on your first car!*

2. <u>Other People's Car Stories:</u> I know someone who is on a limited income, but his daughter wanted a car, so he withdrew funds from his retirement account to buy the expensive sports car she wanted. She did not contribute anything to its purchase. On the other hand, I know a wealthy mother and father who sent their son off to college with the least expensive, full-size car they could find. It cost less than $20,000 new and they had him earn part of the purchase price. Their son contributed to the purchase by working at

a grocery store. *Remember, the best gift you can give your children is the gift of a good example of how to manage their finances responsibly.*

3. How I Buy My Cars Now: When I bought a car a few years ago, the local dealer quoted me a price that I thought was too high. I comparison-shopped at another dealership that had the largest inventory of that make in the state. The second dealer was located some distance away, but the trip was worth it because he offered me a much better price. I showed my local dealer the second dealer's price, and he matched it. *Remember, it pays to comparison shop and use one price against the other.*

4. The How I Chose Real Estate Story: Upon graduating law school, I asked my father what sort of law I should practice as I was having trouble deciding between tax law, tort law, transaction law, banking law, etc. My father, who had only been in California for two weeks; having just bought a manufacturing plant, said, "Go into real estate law; that's where all the money is made in California." I followed his advice and had a very successful and satisfying career as a result. *Remember, when your plans don't go as planned, sometimes something even better is around the corner.*

5. Stanford Tuition Story: My parents offered to pay my tuition to college and law school. They mailed me

the funds each month, but I put their checks in the bank and paid for everything myself. I ran the dormitory laundry, sold ads for and managed the advertising department of the campus newspaper, and ran an off-campus boarding house, but not all at once. When I graduated, I was debt free and had a sizeable nest egg with which to start my career. *Remember, you can learn as much about business from working in the real world as you can from textbooks.*

6. <u>The Riblets Story:</u> At Stanford, I managed an off-campus boarding house. To raise money, I created a profitable weekly social event, an "all you can eat" dinner for about 125 people every Saturday night. We served spaghetti with meat sauce, garlic bread, salad, and a mug full of beer (but the students had to bring their own mug). I bought hamburger in bulk for 10 cents a pound and cheddar cheese for 10 cents a pound. The charge for the dinner was $1.25, but the cost of the food was less than 50 cents per meal. For a change of pace, I once bought lamb riblets on sale for 10 cents a pound, and in order to make them edible, I marinated them overnight in teriyaki soy sauce and broiled them. The boarding house got four orders to a pound and sold them for 25 cents per order. They sold an average of $1.00 worth of riblets to each of the Saturday night guests. Those little riblets added up to big profits by the end of the evening. That was in 1954. *Remember,*

even today, by buying in bulk and being creative with your menu, you can eat well at a reasonable price.

7. The Stanford Alumni Association Story: While at Stanford, I belonged to a club on campus. One year, the club was required to host about 900 people for an alumni reception after one of the football games. The club had only $100 in its bank account. I decided to ask the campus commissary cooks if they had any ideas, and they told me about a beverage flavoring powder we could buy in bulk for about $20. It made enough punch to serve 900 people. We purchased napkins and paper cups at a discount store and spent about $5 on fresh fruit. In those days, $5 could buy quite a few apples, oranges, and peaches. We cut the fruit into small pieces and sprinkled it on top of the punch. The event cost less than $100, within our budget, and the Alumni Association said it was one of the most successfully catered receptions that any campus organization had put on for them! *Remember, for special events, what counts isn't what you spend, it's what people remember.*

8. The Studio Tour Story: I have always loved movies, and my Stanford roommate and I had always wanted to take a tour of a major motion picture studio. In those days, that was only possible if you knew someone. My roommate's mother worked for a studio and she tried to arrange a tour for us,

but she was unable to do so. I was so determined that I wrote a letter to the top executives of each of the three major studios in Hollywood. The letter explained that I was writing an article for the Stanford University newspaper about the influence of motion pictures on college students. I asked for an interview with each studio head and a tour of their studio. All three studios sent me back a pair of private studio tour passes. The heads of two of the studios granted me a personal interview. I sent them copies of the articles after they were published and received access to the studios again the next year! *Remember, "If you can dream it, you can do it."*

9. <u>The Chase Your Losses Story:</u> My grandfather, who was rather successful in the stock market, always warned me that it is basically impossible to know exactly where the top and bottom of the market is. I know a retired couple that were slowly caught up in a huge scam. They started out by initially investing only $13, but slowly, they were conned into sinking their entire life savings of $360,000 into the scam. In the end, all they received was a worthless piece of paper. I have seen others do the same thing with stocks. Instead of being willing to take their losses, they found that it was too painful to their pride to admit a mistake and cut their losses. *Remember, pride is a powerful motivator, but the game called "win back your losses" is a losing game.*

10. The Choose Your Vacations Wisely Story: I know people who take expensive vacations on borrowed money and return from the trip stressed by the debt they have incurred. I also know of two brothers, and one earned only one-fourth of the other. He took vacations economically and locally, while the other one spent lavishly and toured the world. After many years in their respective careers, the brother with the smaller income had a significantly higher net worth because he continued to invest in things of long-term value, rather than in experiences that provide only memories. *Remember, consider the long-term value of your expenditures.*

11. The Car vs. The House Story: I had a client who desperately wanted to own her own home and had set aside savings, but was only $30,000 short of the necessary down payment. She could save the $30,000 she needed over the next four years with her income. She had paid off her car, which was still in excellent condition and would have lasted at least another seven years. One afternoon, she visited a car dealership and allowed a sales associate there to convince her to trade in her paid-off car as a down payment on a new car. Even worse, she didn't agree to buy the new car, she leased it. Now she was locked into monthly lease payments and higher insurance costs for the next four years. What she didn't realize was these additional expenses added up to more than the down payment on a home. In

just one afternoon of not thinking, she had thrown away her opportunity both to own her car and own a home. *Remember, the status of driving a leased luxury car can't be compared to the security of building up equity in a home that you own and a modest car that you own.*

12.   <u>The Walk Around The Farmers Market Story:</u> Almost every weekend, I like to visit local farmers' markets, swap meets, and flea markets. I have discovered that the vendors located nearer the entrance often charge a higher price than those farther away from the entrance. I also check out the prices at the gas stations along the drive to my office. There is often a big difference in the price for the same grade of gas, depending on the location of the station and the brand of gasoline. This can add up to several hundred dollars in savings per year. When I need a big project done at my home or office, I get bids from several vendors and compare the bids. This can save thousands of dollars on the project. *Remember, if people know you comparison shop, and if you ask for a deal, they often will try to give you their best price.*

FAVORITE QUOTES FOR SUCCESS IN LIFE

"The fault, dear Brutus, is not in our stars, but in ourselves."

—*William Shakespeare*

"Most people don't plan to fail; they just fail to plan."

—*Anonymous*

"Expect the best, but plan for the worst."

—*Anonymous*

"You can fool some of the people all of the time, and all of the people some of the time, but you cannot fool all of the people all of the time."

—*Abraham Lincoln*

"Many people take no care of their money 'til they come nearly to the end of it, and others do just the same with their time."

—*Goethe*

"Always do right. This will gratify some people and astonish the rest."

—*Golda Meir*

"Courage is very important. Like a muscle, it's strengthened by use."

—*Muhammad Ali*

"The man who has no imagination has no wings."
                                    —*Norman V. Peale*

"Getting people to like you is simply the other side of liking other people."
                                    —*Mark Twain*

"There are no traffic jams along the extra mile."
                                    —*Roger Staubach*

"A person who never made a mistake never tried anything new."
                                    —*Albert Einstein*

"Either you run the day or the day runs you."
                                    —*Jim Rohn*

"Step by step and the thing is done."
                                    —*Charles Atlas*

"Go for it now. The future is promised to no one."
                                    —*Wayne Dyer*

"All that is necessary for the triumph of evil is that good men do nothing."
                                    —*Edmund Burke*

"It's not what you make; it's what you make of yourself."
                                    —*Samuel K. Freshman*

"We have three things in life to spend: time, energy, and money."

—Anonymous

"Wealth is the ability to fully experience life."

—Henry David Thoreau

"If you buy things you don't need, you are stealing from yourself."

—Czechoslovakian Proverb

"Whoever said money can't buy happiness simply didn't know where to go shopping."

—Bo Derek

"What other people think of you is none of your business."

—Anonymous

"Money may be the husk of many things but not the kernel. It brings you food, but not appetite; medicine, but not health; acquaintance, but not friends; servants, but not loyalty; days of joy, but not peace or happiness."

—Henrik Ibsen

"There are people who have money and people who are rich."

—Coco Chanel

"He is rich or poor according to what he is, not according to what he has."

—*Henry Ward Beecher*

"Money frees you from doing things you dislike. Since I dislike doing nearly everything, money is handy."

—*Groucho Marx*

"Money never makes a man happy yet, nor will it. The more man has, the more he wants. Instead of filling a vacuum, it makes one."

—*Benjamin Franklin*

"He who has enough and doesn't know it is poor."

—*April Benson, Ph.D*

"If a person gets his attitude toward money straight, it will help straighten out almost every other area of his life."

—*Billy Graham*

"The art of living easily as to money is to pitch your scale of living one degree below your means."

—*Sir Richard Taylor*

"If you realize that you're the problem, then you can change yourself, learn something and grow wiser. Don't blame other people for your problems."

—*Robert Kiyosaki*

"If you don't know where you are going, you might wind up someplace else."

—Yogi Berra

"Better to remain silent and be thought a fool then to speak out and remove all doubt."

—Abraham Lincoln

"The best inheritance a parent can give his children is a few minutes of his time each day."

—Orlando A. Battista

"A prudent man foresees the difficulties ahead and prepares for them; the simpleton goes blindly on and suffers the consequences."

—Proverbs 22:3

"The way to get things done is not to mind who gets the credit for doing them."

—Benjamin Jowett

"Your future is created by what you do today, not tomorrow."

—Robert Kiyosaki

"If your desires be endless, your cares and fears will be so too."

—Thomas Fuller

"Our lives improve only when we take chances, and the first and most difficult risk we can take is to be honest with ourselves."

—*Walter Anderson*

"Think big and don't listen to people who tell you it can't be done. Life's too short to think small."

—*Tim Ferris*

"If you want to go somewhere, it is best to find someone who has already been there."

—*Robert Kiyosaki*

"Change is the law of life. And those who look only to the past or present are certain to miss the future."

—*John F. Kennedy*

IF I HAD MY LIFE TO LIVE OVER

(with apologies to Erma Bombeck)

I would have bought more real estate. I would have sold less real estate.

I would have focused more. I would have multi-tasked less.

I would have collected fewer things. I would have given away more things.

I would have listened more closely to parents, teachers, and mentors. I would have listened less to so-called experts.

I would have read more books. I would have watched less television.

I would have written more things down. I would have depended on memory less.

I would have paid more attention to what I ate. I would have paid less attention to how much I ate.

I would have hugged more. I would have shaken hands less.

I would have said "please," "you're welcome," and "thank you" more often. I would have been less impatient, curt, and disrespectful.

I would have complimented more. I would have criticized less.

I would have agreed more. I would have argued less.

I would have been less afraid to ask for what I needed.

I would have been more willing to give to others what they needed.

I would have spent more time with family and friends and my parents. I would have spent less time at the office.

I would have taken more risks.

I would have done more writing.

I would have been at peace more. I would have worried less.

Nevertheless, life has been good to me. It has been a good life.

THE SERENITY PRAYER

God grant me the
Serenity
to accept the things I cannot change, the
Courage
to change the things I can; and the
Wisdom
to know the difference.

SECTION TWO

Principles Of Success
In Business

10 LESSONS MY FATHER TAUGHT ME ABOUT BUSINESS

1. Your family is your first priority.

2. Inflation in the long term is here to stay. Watch the pennies as well as the dollars. Keep all deductible receipts since they are money and worth about 36% or more in real cash. "Since they are money, they are worth about 36 percent or more in real cash when tax time comes."

3. Do not trust the government.

4. Avoid "big hat/no cattle" people who exaggerate their importance.

5. Promise less and deliver more.

6. Listen, listen, listen to your customers and your colleagues.

7. When selling, focus on what your customer wants, not on what you sell.

8. Understand your customers' problems and offer a solution.

9. Beware of attorneys. Use them only when absolutely necessary. Avoid litigation.

10. When speaking to a crowd, visualize everyone with their clothes off and you will feel more relaxed!

10 BUSINESS ETHICS

1. Distinguish between acting based on pride versus acting on principle. Don't say that a mistake was made on principle, when it was really your pride.

2. The customer is always right, until he or she violates your moral code.

3. Consider the long-term ramifications of your actions.

4. Know your personal mission.

5. Know your personal code of ethics.

6. Ask yourself, "How does this action affirm or violate my personal code of ethics?"

7. Always, always take the high road.

8. Be tough, but fair.

9. Don't let unintended slights trigger you to lose your cool.

10. Never lose your sense of humor.

10 WAYS TO GET AHEAD IN YOUR COMPANY

1. Be led by your company's vision.

2. Make your company's mission statement your own.

3. Make your role in the company as creative and productive as possible.

4. Document and share how your efforts contribute to your company's bottom line.

5. Dress and act for the level you want.

6. Do not talk about what other people are earning or the so-called "median" for your position. Most supervisors see this as an excuse for not doing your best.

7. When needed, ask for help. From the right people.

8. Don't say anything to anyone at the office that you wouldn't say to everyone at the office.

9. Watch conversations with co-workers, in and out of the office.

10. Find mentors. Treat them like gold. They are.

20 WAYS TO SUCCEED IN BUSINESS

1. How you think is everything. You become what you think about, and thinking will focus your actions on the subject.

2. Decide upon your goals. Goals should be what you spend most of your thinking time on. Define them objectively and set a time for accomplishment.

3. Act upon goals throughout every day. Have a written action plan with dates for accomplishments.

4. Continue to learn. Take classes, read books, acquire skills. Be creative and explore alternatives.

5. Be persistent and work hard. Get up early. Under promise and over deliver.

6. Plan your day, week, and year.

7. If you do not find problems, you have not looked enough. The secret to success is identifying problems and determining if you can correct them.

8. Focus resources and your time.

9. Communicate effectively orally and in writing. Motivating others requires you to understand their goals rather than your own. Listen more than talk. Do not

be afraid to ask questions when you do not know the answer.

10. Be honest and protect your reputation. It is the only thing that cannot be taken from you.

11. Timing is a critical element in investment success.

12. Be on time and dress for success.

13. You have to know your territory—cold!

14. Do your homework. Be prepared.

15. Take options. Never give them, if you can help it.

16. Rely on your instincts and common sense. If you go against your inner guidance, you usually will regret it.

17. Never lose sight of what business you are in. Stick to your core business.

18. When you suit up each day, it's to play in the major leagues. Think big.

19. Don't remake the wheel. Find new ways of doing things.

20. Focus, persevere, and be ready to change.

10 INVESTMENT PRINCIPLES

1. Never take too much risk. There are always problems. Make sure you plan for them.

2. Decide if an investment is a productive investment or an "ego" investment.

3. Success is 90 percent preparation and 10 percent perspiration. But both are necessary. Take risks that are carefully researched and calculated.

4. A great idea without effective execution is simply a great idea.

5. Watch for opportunities, be prepared to act on opportunities, and have the courage to seize opportunities.

6. An entrepreneur must be prudent and careful in spending in order to have capital when opportunity presents itself.

7. The seven words that lead to loss of market share are, "We have always done it that way." But remember New Coke and Allegis. Change, solely for the sake of change, without a purpose and a test, is, at best, a sunk cost, and at worst, a loss of market share.

8. The whole "dot.com" culture was based on the postponement of gratification. That is, the trading of salaries for stock options. MBAs could go to Wall Street in merger and acquisition positions and make $75,000 to $150,000 a year, or go to work for the new dot.com companies for $1,000 to $2,000 a month, if there is a stock option program where they have a chance to become millionaires. They are basically betting that the company will be successful. I invest with entrepreneurs who are willing to postpone gratification, thus tying their success to the success of the company. Compensation should not be front-end loaded.

9. Wall Street wants to raise large sums of money. They couldn't care less about entrepreneurs for two reasons: it is not their money, and they are playing the result (like a casino, they win either way). This is the key to the private placement internet funds. They get 20% of the upside and none of the downside, so if they invest in five companies, and one is a winner, two break even, and two are complete losses, then they are way ahead.

10. Analyze details. The winner in most every transaction is the one most prepared. Set out a list of information you need to acquire for your project to be a success, continue to ask questions, and determine every detail that needs to be checked to be sure you are on the right track.

10 TIPS ON WORKING WITH PEOPLE

1. Hire people who have more knowledge than you on the subject. Use caution in hiring friends, relatives, and everyone else.

2. Be aware that middle managers sometimes hire mediocrity to protect their position.

3. Everyone is important, but no one is indispensable. That being said, be sure you always can reach your key associates anytime, anywhere, and any place.

4. The phrase, "loose lips sink ships" is true. Stress confidentiality.

5. Find and delegate people who are more skilled at tasks that are not your unique ability. This makes your job easier.

6. Attitude is more important than skill. Surround yourself with people who have a positive attitude.

7. Don't try to change people; people usually do not change.

8. The difference between a successful organization and an unsuccessful organization is more often not capital or years in business, but its people.

9. Find out where people are coming from, and what is their professional background and motivation. The only way to find out is to ask. If you don't ask, you won't know.

10. Think before answering. When unsure, consider and consult. Avoid pride. Avoid anger. Anger is a result of our own errors. Don't lose your sense of humor.

WHAT I HAVE LEARNED FROM BEING A...

1. **Board Chairman:** Start board meetings on time. Keep board meetings focused on problem solving. Prepare your agenda and stick to it. If the discussion starts to stray, refer the issue to a committee.

2. **Borrower:** You need to shop for competitive bids for loans, just as you do for any other product. It's the banker, not the bank, that determines the outcome.

3. **Business Partner:** Have strong compatibility with your business partner. Make sure that you and your partner are willing to share in the decision making.

4. **College Professor and Lecturer:** The instructor often learns more from the students than they do from him or her.

5. **Horseback Rider:** Sometimes the horse knows better than you.

6. **Husband, Father, Grandfather:** Always be available for your family, be sensitive to their needs, and look for opportunities for quality time together.

7. **Networker:** Always carry business cards.

8. <u>**Overnight Camp Counselor:**</u> Keep your campers busy, learning, and most importantly, having fun.

9. <u>**Public Speaker:**</u> Give the audience what they came to hear, not what you came to sell.

10. <u>**Lender:**</u> Be cautious about anyone who offers more than the current market rate.

20 TIPS FOR MANAGING PEOPLE

1. Plan your day, your week, your year, and your career.

2. Give compliments liberally.

3. Criticize in private. Never criticize a person, criticize the action.

4. Praise in public. Praise employees and associates. Give credit to those who merit it.

5. Delegate when possible. Provide oversight.

6. Be available for coaching. Encourage education.

7. Investigate and verify when there is a dispute.

8. Simplify procedures.

9. Do not hide problems, face them squarely.

10. A true leader is accessible—no job too big, no job too small.

11. Promote integrity, honesty and responsibility.

12. Don't hide bad news. Bring it up and talk it through.

13. Admit mistakes. Learn from them. Don't repeat them.

14. Under promise, over deliver.

15. Listen to employees and clients. Meet their needs.

16. Show respect to everyone.

17. Encourage innovation.

18. Teamwork is what it takes to win.

19. Loyalty to the company is a necessary virtue.

20. Have fun.

"DEAL JUNKY" HUMOROUS STORIES

1. <u>The Elephant Story:</u> At a recent real estate trade convention, I was approached by a broker from Columbus, Ohio (with whom I had done a number of deals) who told me she had a wonderful opportunity for me. One of her close, personal friends who she went to nursery school with was willing to sell me his pet elephant. Of course, it was only because of this relationship that she could offer me this deal; the elephant could be mine for merely $10,000. She suggested the elephant would be a great attraction for my shopping centers. I carefully explained that I had no place to keep an elephant, that it would require an elephant trainer and I could not think of a way to get rid of the elephant poop. She then indicated that she might be able to get the price down to as low as $100. I repeated my objections to acquiring an elephant. Finally, after much discussion, she said, "Look, I believe I can get my friend to give it to you for free." I again repeated my objections to her for acquiring an elephant. In desperation, she said, "I believe he has two of them." I replied, "Let's talk." *Remember to not say "yes" right away.*

2. <u>The Sardine Story:</u> I had a neighbor who was a wholesale grocer. At the time, there was a shortage of sardines, and I asked him if he could get me a case for a party I was planning. My neighbor said

that he had a warehouse full of sardines and he would be happy to sell me some. The price was rising, greed stepped in, and I bought 100 cases. My wife asked me to bring home a case, and when we opened it, the sardines looked beautiful. However, when we went to eat them, they were too bitter. In a panic, I called my neighbor and told him that I was very upset with him dumping bad sardines on me. He asked, "What did you try to do with them?" I replied, "Eat them." He explained patiently, "Those aren't eating sardines, those are trading sardines!" *Remember that it is not a bargain if you cannot use it.*

3. **The Flood Story:** Bob retired and went to Miami Beach to enjoy his later years. One day, while sunning himself in front of his hotel, a gentleman laid down a blanket, stretched out, and started a conversation with him. Bob introduced himself to the gentleman, and in the conversation, Bob mentioned," I had a clothing business, and after a fire, I collected the insurance and I retired to Miami." The gentleman said, "I can top that. I had a bakery business, I had a flood, I collected my insurance, and I retired to Miami." Bob turned to the gentleman and inquired, "How do you make a flood?" *Remember that there is always someone who has a better story than you do.*

4. <u>**The True Believer:**</u> A true believer in God lived by the Mississippi River. During the last flood season, his home was in the path of the flood and he had to climb to the roof. As water reached the level of the roof, a neighbor came by in a rowboat and offered to take him to safety. He replied, "God will provide," and waived the neighbor off. About an hour later, as the water came up to his knees, a launch came by with Red Cross workers who again offered to take him off the roof. He sent them away, saying, "God will provide." Finally, as the water was reaching up to his chest level, a sheriff's helicopter came by and dropped a ladder. He shouted up to them, "God will provide" and told them he didn't need help. As the water came up to his chin, he looked up to the heavens and shouted, "God, why have you forsaken me?" A voice boomed down from the heavens and said, "Who do you think sent the row boat, the launch, and the helicopter?" *Remember to take help when it is offered, because God helps those who help themselves.*

5. <u>**The Moose Hunt Story:**</u> Two real estate developer friends of mine, Phil and Bill, fly up to Northern Canada every year to hunt moose. They take Air Canada to Toronto, where they meet a pilot with a small pontoon equipped plane to fly them to a lake just below Hudson's Bay. Upon meeting the pilot, they make arrangements for the pilot to pick them back up at the end of the week's stay in the moose

country. The pilot flies them up and a guide comes out in a canoe to pick them up. The pilot tells them, "Remember, this plane can only carry one moose, plus the three of us out of this small lake." They reply that they understand. When the pilot returns in a week to pick them up, the guide brings them out in a canoe, trailed by another canoe with two dead moose. The pilot reminds them that the plane can only carry one moose. They assure the pilot that if he goes up to the edge of the lake and guns the motor, he can clear the pines at the other edge of the lake. They agree to pay him $5,000 for the attempt. The pilot, whose wife needs a special operation and is in desperate need for money, reluctantly agrees. The pilot backs up to the edge of the lake, guns the motor, takes off, and immediately crashes into the pines and the plane drops like a stone to the ground. As Bill and Phil stumble out of the wreckage, Bill says to Phil, "Where the hell are we?" Phil replies, "Only about 500 feet beyond where we crashed last year." *Remember Einstein said that doing the same thing over and over and expecting different results is insane.*

6. **The Horse Trader Story:** Ike and Mike were horse traders and good friends. Ike sold Mike a beautiful horse for $2,500, but it had one bad leg. After a few weeks, Ike wondered why Mike had not called him to complain about the bad leg. His curiosity got the best of him, so Ike called Mike and asked, "How's

the horse?" Mike replied, "It has one bad leg, but it did have three good ones." Ike said, "What did you do with it?" Mike said, "I sold eight tickets in a raffle for it at $1,000 each." Ike asked, "What did you do when the winner complained?" Mike said, "It was simple, Ike. I just gave him his money back." *Remember that a good horse trader can make money on a lame horse.*

7. <u>The Scorpion and the Frog:</u> A frog and a scorpion approached a river they needed to cross. The scorpion said to the frog, "Let me get on your back and carry us both across the river." The frog replied, "I can't do that. You will sting me and I will drown." The scorpion said, "That doesn't make any sense. If I sting you, we will both drown." The frog thought it over and told the scorpion, "That makes sense. I will carry you across." The scorpion hopped on the frog's back, and when they reached the middle of the river, the scorpion stung the frog and they both started to drown. The frog exclaimed, "Why did you do that?" The Scorpion looked at the frog and told him, "I couldn't help it; it's my nature." *Remember that people don't change.*

8. <u>The Banker's Shirt Story:</u> The local banker was the greediest person in town. Jane was the owner of the largest store in town. She loved to make bets with her friends. One evening, she was playing cards with her friend, John, the local doctor. The topic of the

banker came up and Jane said, "I bet I can get him to take off his shirt in his office!" John replied, "I'll bet you $10,000 you can't get him to do it!" Jane exclaimed, "You're on!" She made an appointment the next day to visit the banker, telling his secretary she and John had an important business transaction for him. As they were ushered in, the banker said, "What can I do for you?" Jane answered, "I bet John $10,000 that you wouldn't take off your shirt in front of us." The banker, seeing an opportunity to make a quick $5,000, said, "Well you are wrong!" and immediately took off his shirt. Then John sheepishly opened his wallet and gave $10,000 to Jane, who in turn handed $5,000 to the banker. *Remember, people can be very cooperative when you share the profits.*

9. <u>**The Dress Maker Story (Part 1):**</u> Hal was the most successful dress manufacturer in the city. He sold his company to a corporation. At his retirement dinner, his major competitor asked, "Hal, your line always outsells ours. How do you decide what fashions to run?" Hal said, "This works every time. I call in my wife and daughter and we look at all the design choices for the next season. Whatever my wife and daughter like, we scrap. Whatever they don't like, we run!" *Remember to sell what your customer wants, not what you want.*

10. <u>The Dress Maker Story (Part 2):</u> Nick and Rick were partners in a small dress making business. Their facility was on the 13th floor, while Hal, the most successful dressmaker in town, had his facility on the 21st floor. Nick and Rick were nearly bankrupt, so they decided that one of them would have to commit suicide so the other partner could collect the life insurance. They drew straws. Nick lost the draw, climbed the stairs to the roof of their building, and jumped. As he was falling, he passed Hal's window and saw what Hal was manufacturing. As Nick flew past the 13th floor, he yelled to Rick, "Use cut-velvet!" *Remember to be aware of what your competition is doing.*

11. <u>The "Ethical" Judge Story:</u> A small-town judge had been on the bench for many years and had a reputation for fairness, all because of what he had said at the beginning of his first trial. That morning, he had announced, "Last night, the plaintiff in this case took me to dinner and gave me $5,000 to decide the case in his favor. This morning, the defendant in this case took me to breakfast and gave me $10,000 to decide the case in his favor. Let the record show that I am returning $5,000 to the defendant and I will decide the case on its merits." *Remember to make sure the dollars add up right.*

12. <u>The Doctor and Lawyer Story:</u> A doctor and lawyer, who were both friends, attended a dinner party. At

the party, one of the doctor's patients came up to him and engaged him in a ten-minute conversation concerning legal advice that the patient wanted. The doctor complained to his friend, the lawyer, that there must be something the doctor could do about that. The lawyer said the answer was simple. Send him a bill tomorrow for medical advice. The doctor replied, "That's an excellent suggestion. I will do so." The next morning, the doctor received a bill from the lawyer "for legal advice to send a bill to your patient: $100." *Remember to be careful from whom you ask advice.*

13.   **The Bank Teller Story:** Henry Sullivan carried a large briefcase as he walked into a bank and approached the new accounts desk. He said, "I want to see John Smith, the president of the bank, about opening a major account. The officer phoned the president and instructed Sullivan to go down the hall and to the right. "I know," he said. When Sullivan entered the president's office, he opened his briefcase and dumped $1 million in cash onto the desk. (This was before the current anti-money laundering laws!) The president gasped, looked closely at Sullivan, and asked, "Don't I know you?" Sullivan exclaimed, "Yes! I was a teller here ten years ago! You fired me and told me I would never amount to anything!" The president then asked, "If I fired you, why are you giving me $1 million?" Sullivan replied, "If you hadn't fired me, I would still be a teller." *Remember*

that when one door closes, another one may be opening.

14. <u>The Fire Engine Story:</u> A suburban chemical company had a large fire and all the cities sent their brand new fire equipment and teams consisting of firefighters in their 20s to mid-30s. The heat was very intense and the fire departments hesitated to enter the factory compound. The owner of the chemical plant announced that it had valuable packs in the company's safe and whoever was successful in putting out the fire would receive a check for $100,000. Still, no one entered the plant area. Suddenly, from a distance, they heard an old-time fire bell. An old fire engine roared up and into the plant compound at a high rate of speed. On the side of the fire truck was the name of the local retirement community volunteer fire department. A group of 60- to 80-year-old firefighters jumped off the truck and put out the fire. At the celebration dinner, a check for $100,000 was handed to the chief of the retirement community volunteer fire department. The chief of the local city fire department raised his hand and asked if he could make an inquiry. The volunteer chief said, "Of course." The city chief inquired, "We admire the work of your volunteer fire department. What are you going to do with the money?" The volunteer chief replied, "The first thing we will do is fix the brakes on our fire truck!"

Remember that what may appear to be heroic may simply be a matter of circumstances.

15. <u>The Ring Story:</u> Pat and his partner, Matt, met for lunch every day at the jewelry mart, as business had been slow. Pat said to Matt, "I have always admired your ring. Why don't you sell it to me? I will give you $5,000." Matt said, "Okay!" The deal is sealed and the ring and check exchanged hands. The next day, Matt said to Pat, "I really think I sold that ring too cheap, I will buy it back for $5,500." The ring and check exchanged hands again. The following day, Pat said to Matt, "You know I really love that ring. I will give you $6,000." The ring and check exchanged hands once again. After a considerable period of time, the price of the ring grew to $10,000. They met for lunch, and it was Matt's turn to offer to buy the ring from Pat. Matt presented his check for $10,500. Pat replied, "Matt, I am sorry, but I sold the ring to a customer yesterday for $10,500." Matt exclaimed, "How could you sell that ring when we were both making such a good living out of it?!" *Remember to not confuse activity with real profit.*

PERSONAL STORIES
ABOUT BUSINESS

1. <u>Hong Kong Tailor Story:</u> For a recent trip to Hong Kong, our travel agent suggested that we have some clothes made and gave us the name of a tailor. At the tailor's office, we were ushered into a lounge and offered coffee or tea. The salesman explained that a great deal of time went into selecting the perfect fabric for each suit. He said that special cloth patterns are chosen to match the client's personality, and then an order is sent to the Shetland Islands for the wool. Once the wool has been taken from the sheep, it then goes to Manchester, England, where it would be woven into cloth. The woven cloth is then sent back to Hong Kong to be sewn and cut to the proper measurements. I informed him that I would have to buy the suit the next time we came to Hong Kong because we were leaving the next morning for Shanghai." The salesman replied, "I will deliver the suit to your hotel tonight!" *Remember to do what has to be done to make the sale.*

2. <u>The House Sale Story:</u> I was planning to move from Beverly Hills to Malibu and had put our house up for sale. We had lived in it for approximately 20 years while our four daughters were growing up. I was on an overnight trip in Omaha to look at an industrial park. At 11 p.m., I was awakened by an unexpected phone call. It from was the head of a major movie

studio that is a household word. He announced, "I am interested in your house and understand you are asking $1,200,000. I will pay you $1,000,000." I politely said, "Thank you for the offer, but that price won't work." He informed me that, "Everyone in Beverly Hills sells their house for less than their asking price." So I would understand his urgency, he shared two pieces of information. First, he revealed that he needed occupancy within 10 days. I asked, "Why do you need occupancy within 10 days?" He replied that he had already sold his house and had to get out in 10 days. Then he revealed why he had to have our house. He said, "My wife is driving me crazy. She believes your house is the one we must buy." I thought for a moment and replied, "I will move out of our house in 10 days. But only if you agree to pay the full price." And we did and he did. *Remember to not disclose that you have no alternative when negotiating a purchase.*

3. <u>The Candy Store Story:</u> In my hometown, there were two local candy stores. One is known as "the good" candy store and the other is known as "the bad" candy store. Both candy stores charged the same price per pound for their candy, gave their customers the same amount of candy in a pound, and sold the same quality of candy. In the "bad" candy store, the propriety used a large scoop to place the candy on a scale and then subtracted some of the candy until a pound was reached. In the "good" candy

store, the proprietor used a small scoop to place the candy on the scale and added candy until a pound was reached. *Remember that perception is as important as reality.*

4. <u>The Jewelry Story:</u> My personal jeweler, Pat, has provided me with many great "deals" on estate jewelry. The deals may be the oddly shaped, out-of-style pieces that my wife refuses to wear. She criticizes me for acquiring them. Later, when they come into style again, she wears them often and admires them. *Remember, think before you reject something. You may want it later.*

5. <u>The Yangtze River Trip Story:</u> We were on a trip to China and booked a five-day tour on a river steamer. We were told by our guide to ask for a deluxe accommodations upgrade since the standard accommodation would not be satisfactory. On board, a steward was assigned to take our luggage to our room. As instructed, we asked the steward to show us a deluxe room that was about $250 higher than the standard room. After seeing the deluxe room, I asked if there was anything better and he said, "We do have two large suites." He showed us the suites, which were five times bigger than the deluxe rooms and had private decks. I asked the price and was told, "These suites are $1,500." As the boat was pulling out of the dock and we were already into the main part of the river, my question

to the steward was, "What happens to those suites if I don't take one?" He answered, "They will be empty for the balance of the trip." My reply was, "I will give you $500 for a suite." The steward said, "That is much less than what we asked, but I can consult with the captain." I replied, "Please do so." The steward came back in a few minutes and said, "The suite is yours." *Remember in negotiating to not be too quick to close a deal.*

6. <u>The Picture Frame Story:</u> My father-in-law, Ben, was the manager of the art supply department in several May Company Department stores. They often ran specials on picture frames. He told me of the following experience. A customer came in and asked to buy three frames for $5. My father-in-law replied, "Our special is two frames for $5, not three." The customer said, "Your competitor down the street is offering three frames for $5." Ben replied, "Why don't you buy from them?" The customer said, "They don't have any." Ben stated, "When we don't have any frames to sell, we offer them four for $5." *Remember that it's not a bargain if it's not available.*

7. <u>The Capsule Story:</u> I learned to look for real value when I was young. Once, I visited my cousin who was working as a butcher in a supermarket. In the display case was ground sirloin for $1.50 per pound and hamburger for $1.00 per pound. I asked my cousin, the butcher, "What is the difference between

the ground sirloin and the hamburger?" He replied, "Honestly, 50 cents a pound." My father was a manufacturer of vitamins for most of the major drug chains on the West Coast. One of his customers was a high-end pharmacy that sold his multi-vitamin formula in a green capsule for $16 a bottle. Another customer was a large chain of discount drug stores. They sold the same multi-vitamins in a red capsule for $8 a bottle. Each bottle contained the same number of capsules. I once asked my father, "What is the difference between what the pharmacy is selling and what the discount drug store is selling?" He replied simply, "One capsule is green and the other is red." *Remember that the most expensive is not always better than the less expensive.*

8. <u>The Cantaloupe Story:</u> When I was young during my summers in Michigan, my father negotiated with local growers to allow my brothers and me to pick cantaloupes and watermelons left behind by the harvesters in the nearby fields. Then we would go door-to-door selling the produce we had gathered in those fields and in our own backyard garden to our neighbors. *Remember, there is value lying around, if you are willing to use a little effort to pick it up.*

9. <u>The First Office Story:</u> When I first started practicing law, I had the goal of an office in Beverly Hills, but I couldn't find "a space for services" arrangement,

to exchange my legal time in exchange for office space. (This was how most young lawyers started back then, when they did not have enough money to rent an office.) I did, however, find a firm that had a large, windowless storeroom. It rented for only $25 a month, compared to the average rate of $100 a month for an office with a window. When I bought my office furniture, I asked the furniture store decorator for advice. The decorator suggested installing drapes across one of the walls to give the impression that a window was behind the drapes. I followed this advice, and thus created a presentable office within my budget. *Remember, you can have (almost) what you want, if you are willing to be creative.*

10. <u>The Toothpaste Story:</u> Years ago, I hired a new attorney who sometimes seemed overly impressed with the large sums of money necessary to complete the real estate deals for our company. During a high-powered meeting out of town, I put a $1,000,000 cashier's check on the table. The meeting took longer than anticipated, so we had to find a hotel and buy a few supplies at the drug store. The attorney stood in line at the checkout counter with a hairbrush, toothbrush, and toothpaste. I was standing in line with a comb, toothbrush, and toothpaste, and I told the attorney, "All you need is the toothbrush and a comb, which costs 10% of the price of that hairbrush. You can come over to my

room and use my toothpaste." I did this to make a point, little knowing that more than 20 years later, the lawyer, who went on to become very successful, would recount the story at a banquet celebrating his success. *Remember, you never know how your example can make a difference in other people's lives.*

TIME EFFICIENCY AND EFFECTIVENESS TIPS

Choose one technique from each category and try it. If you need to develop a habit, practice it for 21 days. After you have attained mastery, savor that impetus and attempt a new technique.

Meetings

1. When you attend a meeting, make a list of the follow-up action steps you will need to take after the meeting and the target completion dates of each action step. If you leave the meeting without a list, ask yourself if attending the meeting was a good use of your time.

2. When you hold a meeting, demonstrate that you will respect everyone's time. Distribute an agenda ahead of the meeting, with estimated time for each topic. Announce that the meeting will start and end on time ("cell phone time").

3. Foster efficiency at the meeting. Try brief, daily, stand-up meetings, or meet during lunch or breakfast. Go around the room and have each person give a two-sentence or two-minute update on their goals or progress. Set a timer for each update so they will be succinct.

4. Follow-up: At the end of every meeting, get feed-back on how the meeting went and how it could have been improved. Make sure that everyone leaves the meeting with a specific, individual commitment to a plan of action and a deadline for completion. Arrange for highlights of the meeting, including this information, to be distributed to everyone who attended and those who could not attend.

Communicating With Others

1. Online: Smart phones allow you to get your emails away from your computer. Acknowledge each email as soon as it is read, even if it is a quick: "Thanks, okay, maybe, let me check," or "I'll get back to you on that." If possible, do not check for emails continually. They can be very distracting. It is better to check your email only at scheduled periods during the day, such as at 10 a.m. and 3 p.m., or between your appointments. Let people know what those times are, so they know when they can expect a response.

2. Use good "netiquette." Do not use all caps (this de-notes yelling). Use lots of courtesy, such as "I apol-ogize," "please," and "thank you." Hurt feelings and hidden sabotage take much more time to fix than the time it takes to be extra courteous. However, make your point clearly and ask a specific question or request a specific action at the end of your email.

3. Keep phone calls courteous, but brief and to the point. People will be more inclined to take your call and return your call if they know you will be brief. If you cannot reach someone by phone, always leave a message or a voice message. It is annoying to know that someone called, but did not leave a message. Your message should include a specific request and the best time for a return call. Use email for requests that need documentation and are not time-sensitive. Use phone calls when a back-and-forth conversation would help you make a complicated decision or when you need to strengthen your connection with that person. Use one-on-one meetings for situations that require more than a phone call.

4. Use good etiquette during one-on-one meetings. The person talking to you deserves more respect than the person trying to email, text, or phone you. Otherwise, you are wasting their time and insulting them. Give your undivided attention to the person who went to the trouble to see you in person.

Daily Efficiency

1. Allow for new ideas by keeping a pad of paper by your bed, in the bathroom, and in the kitchen. Write down ideas as soon as they come to you so you don't have to remember them. Use drive time and exercise time for brainstorming or listening to books on tape.

2. Consider your commute time. Try to find an office that is close to your home and convenient for your clients. It should be close to a good restaurant where you can entertain your clients. Choose an athletic club that is close to your office or your home.

3. Organize your life. Have a place for everything and put everything in its place. Looking for misplaced items is a waste of time and money. Designate separate binders and files for each client or project. Toss, file, delegate, or schedule each piece of paper. Tear out pages; don't keep the whole publication. Keep checklists for recurring events such as meetings and trips. Create template form letters and office materials. Cross reference and make duplicates of important information.

4. Be decisive. Do you need to consult with someone else first?

5. Use the Pareto Principle, that 20 percent of effort produces 80 percent of results. Ask yourself, "What should I be doing right now?

6. Develop routines. Make it a routine to get up, dress up, and show up each day. What tasks do you do daily? Put them on autopilot. Make to-do lists, lay out your clothes, and pack your briefcase the night before. You can take advantage of opportunities if you are prepared.

7. Schedule your day. Determine what three big projects must be done that day for the day to be considered successful. Keep a list of those projects, along with the necessary emails and phone calls. First, make the calls or tackle the tasks that you are uncomfortable doing, perhaps because of a fear of rejection.

8. Schedule more time than anticipated. Schedule extra time for traveling to and from meetings. In your calendar, post the time that you need to leave for a meeting, in addition to the time you need to arrive at the meeting.

9. Respect your privacy. If you need privacy to complete a task, ask for it.

10. Respect your time. Put boundaries around your time. When you are asked to do something extra that you cannot do, learn to say, "I'm sorry, I can't," or "No, that task would be better for someone else to do." Respect the schedules of the other people in your life and coordinate with them.

11. Write down your personal and professional goals. Share them with stakeholders. Break down your long-term goals into monthly, weekly, and daily tasks. Make specific goals for each of your many roles, such as parent, spouse, son/daughter, employer/employee, sibling, friend, community member, etc.

Make sure you are giving sufficient attention to each of your roles.

12. Set aside needed time, such as an appointment with yourself that you keep as if you were meeting with your boss. If you are procrastinating, ask yourself what you are avoiding.

13. Separate urgent from important. Try to prevent urgent crises by being proactive. When a crisis occurs, figure out how to prevent it from recurring. Ask yourself, what is the worst-case scenario? Focus on important, long-term goals. Spend time on planning how to create more time.

Also see: *How to Get Control of Your Time and Your Life* by Allen Laykin, www.TaylorInTime.com and www. DavidCo.com.

15 NETWORKING TIPS

1. Use trade associations; work within them.

2. Find a common interest and share information about it.

3. Start at the top. You can always work your way down.

4. Business and personal networking require different approaches.

5. Do personal networking one-to-one. Face time makes all the difference.

6. People who are shy should use networking organizations, such as Toastmasters, Chambers of Commerce, etc., to develop networking skills.

7. Join networking groups like Vistage, YPO, Provisors, and Tiger21. There are useful peer groups that span cultural and geographic boundaries.

8. The problem with networking skills is that some people need to learn them, but don't, while other people learn them and use them too aggressively.

9. At mixers and professional events, allow plenty of time to travel to the event, park, and find the right room. When you arrive early, you create a favorable

impression with the host and you have time to mingle before the event.

10. Make notes on the back of business cards you receive. This will remind you to call or send more information.

11. If you attend with friends or colleagues, split up. Divide and conquer. Sit at different tables so you can meet as many new people as possible.

12. Your business card should be easy to read and give all necessary information, including your email address and website. Keep a lot of your business cards wrapped in a rubber band in your pocket, along with a pen.

13. Always be ready. Any occasion can be an opportunity to network, including social events. Have your business cards and a pen in your pocket at all times. I have made some of my best contacts waiting at the valet stand or waiting for an elevator.

14. Know your elevator speech by heart. Always be ready to ask what the other person does and tell them what you do. When I introduce myself to someone, I say my name, shake hands, exchange, pleasantries, and then ask, "What do you do?" Then I know what to say regarding what I do.

15. Have a specific prospect profile. Only certain kinds of people will help increase your business. For example, I am looking for people who want to buy or sell real estate, want real estate loans, or need me as an expert witness in real estate litigation. I look for homeowners or people with companies that need my water treatment company. I am also looking for people in real estate who graduated from my alma mater, Stanford University and Stanford Law School, to join Stanford Professionals in Real Estate (SPIRE) of which I am chairman emeritus

For further information, read *How To Win Friends and Influence People* by Dale Carnegie.

FINANCING CASE STUDIES

Principle: Think Outside the Box

1. A borrower had a lease on a special purpose property that gave the borrower the option to buy during the lease. The property had increased in value to where the borrower's option was 70% of the value. A lender was identified who would make the loan, but the lender required the equity to be valued at cost. The lender could not fund 100% of the total cost. At the time, the property would support a loan of 100% of total option cost on a value basis, but the borrower could not show cost equity. The borrower's mortgage broker brought him to me. After a review of the circumstances, I renegotiated the lease to provide that a portion of previous paid rental payments were allocated toward an increased purchase price to provide the cost ratio that the lender required. Upon receiving the revised lease, the lender agreed to fund the project.

2. An insurance company wanted to buy a building which was owned by a probate estate for the purchase of a headquarters building. The estate was in litigation, and liquidation was being held up by a creditor whose claim was modest in relation to the assets of the estate. The state insurance department examiner was going to disallow the building as an asset of the insurance company, unless it could pro-

duce a title policy for ownership of the building. I was retained to solve the problem. Title policies are normally written to insure record title. I convinced a title insurer to issue a special form of surety policy, guaranteeing the return of the advance if the title was not ultimately secured from the estate within a specific period of time, and I convinced the state insurance department to accept it.

3. A non-profit hospital wanted to provide a medical office building for its staff on the land it owned. It did not have the equity required to build a building, so I arranged a lease of the land to a syndicate of staff doctors, who provided the equity and built the building.

4. Some individuals wanted to build a hospital. I arranged for 100% financing by negotiating key money from concessions, such as a pharmacy, a laboratory, a hospital supply company, etc. The funding created from the key money and syndication gave them two-thirds of the hospital equity with no investment.

5. A mortgage broker approached me to arrange a hard-money loan for his client, who was buying a house in an expensive residential area. The client needed a second loan of about $400,000. The broker had proposed a second mortgage at 10 points and 10% interest. In reviewing the borrower's financial statement, I determined that the borrower was a

composer who had residuals that would support a bank loan. I arranged for a first mortgage loan on the residuals at a fraction of the cost of the second mortgage loan.

6. I acquired two buildings that had short-term high amortization loans. I refinanced one and syndicated equity in the other one for enough to pay for the equity on both.

7. A borrower with a high net worth needed a $20,000,000 construction loan and had an $18,000,000 bank commitment. I arranged for a $2,000,000 letter of credit on the borrower's signature and the lender increased the loan to $20,000,000. The borrower initially had considered getting a second mortgage at 12%. The letter of credit was for 3%, thus saving the borrower $180,000.

8. A tax attorney who attended one of my lectures came up after the lecture and asked me if I knew of a bank which would lend her and her husband $300,000 on a construction loan for a house they were building. The total cost of the house was $700,000 and they had already purchased the property, which they owned free and clear, for $400,000. Their plan was to finish the house and get a permanent loan. They were having difficulty getting the loan and had consulted a number of banks that had quoted them substantial fees for appraisals and inspections, as

well as points for the loan. I looked at their financial statements. Her husband was also a successful attorney, and I determined that they would be good commercial bank customers. We restructured their request from a construction loan for a one-year commercial loan at an interest rate equivalent to the construction loan rate, but without the appraisal fees, points etc. This eliminated a lot of paperwork and saved them several thousand dollars by placing the loan with a local bank that was interested in having a lawyer-based clientele.

Principle: Have An Alternative

9. A major sports team's franchise was negotiating with a city for the use of their stadium. The franchise had done a feasibility study and determined that this stadium was the best location. The city required the personal guarantee of the team owner for a number of years and a parking rate which would have placed a financial strain on the operation. The owner wanted to go forward, but was reluctant to sign the guarantee and had concern over the parking rate. Through my personal contacts, I negotiated a lease proposal with another city for the use of its stadium on a basis of no personal guarantee and a lower parking cost. These negotiations, through carefully chosen contacts, were "leaked" to the negotiating personnel of the target city. The result was a lease

executed with the target city on the terms desired by the owner.

10. A Midwest theater chain planned a seven-year bond issue of $100,000,000 for renovation and expansion at 13% and $4,000,000 in costs. I proposed a combined bank and insurance company credit facility of $100,000,000, with a $67,000,000 initial disbursement, and additional advances as cash flow grew at a lower rate, and at $2,000,000 in costs. The total savings would be over $20,000,000 in interest and loan costs over the term, plus more flexibility.

11. A long-time client in the hotel business wanted to replace mezzanine financing. I was able to cut the interest rate the client was paying in half by restructuring the loan and changing lenders.

Principle: Find Out What The Client Really Needs

12. A hospital partnership acquired land subject to a mortgage. The mortgage had been executed by the seller. The mortgage contained a prohibition against prepayment. The owner of the mortgage refused to accept prepayment, blocking a loan for the construction. The mortgage was in an amount below the land value ($600,000 vs. $1,000,000 that was paid for the land). I negotiated with a title

insurance company to hold securities that produced income sufficient to make mortgage payments and principal on maturity of the existing mortgage. The title company agreed to delete the mortgage from its policy, and the lender agreed to make the loan. The title policy held the lender harmless from the existing mortgage.

Principle: Get a Financial Partner

13. Some borrowers had a property that they owned free and clear and used as a parking lot for an adjoining building that contained various amenities, such as a pool and a tennis court. The borrowers wanted to erect a luxury apartment building on the parking lot and use the amenities in the adjoining building (which building was subject to a separate loan) for the apartment building. They had been attempting for four years to secure financing. The borrowers' track record and credit were not sufficient to secure the new loan necessary. Their mortgage broker brought them to me and I became a co-developer. I restructured the loan application, eliminating cross easements by refinancing the existing building as part of the package for the new project. I also renegotiated the construction contracts and architecture contracts and assisted in revising and improving the design. As a result of my involvement, construction and take-out loans were secured in approximately

four months. The project was successfully completed for a total cost of $50,000,000 and was resold a few months later for more than $80,000,000.

14. A small, West Coast theater chain had the opportunity to secure a long-term leasehold on a "no brainier" location with a very high payback probability. It was estimated that the cost of the theater could be recovered in approximately five years, as the location had no competition at the time. The landlord was willing to supply the shell of the building rent free for 20 years, as it needed a theater to stabilize the rest of the project. This was the only location in the area with sufficient parking. The landlord did not have the funds to build out a theater. The landlord was concerned that the chain had sufficient credit and resources to complete the theatre and required a strong financial statement. The theater operator did not have the credit to convince the landlord to execute the lease or secure the necessary funding, so I became a co-developer and owner. The $3,000,000 required to build out and equip the theater was secured, repayable over five years from commercial banks for the venture. The landlord executed the lease, the theater was built, and rather than taking approximately four to five years to pay off the financing, the cash flow paid off the financing in approximately 30 months.

15. Some borrowers had an apartment building that they had constructed, and at the time of completion, did not create sufficient rental to support the loan of approximately $9,000,000. The borrowers were able to place the property into Chapter 11 and held off the lender for several years. During this time, the rental increased to the point where the best loan the borrowers could secure was an 8.75% interest rate with 1.2 coverage that did not give them the sufficient funds to discharge the loan. My involvement in the project enabled them to secure a loan at approximately 6.8%, which on a 1.2 coverage ratio, would cover almost all the amount necessary to pay off the creditors. I provided mezzanine financing for the small balance.

A 10-STEP COURSE ON LAW

1. If a proposal is too good to be true, it probably is.

2. Read the small print and the footnotes.

3. Use attorneys when necessary to avoid litigation.

4. Offer less than you are sure you can deliver.

5. Don't do or say anything you don't want to see in the newspaper.

6. Deal with the press and make public statements cautiously.

7. If there is a problem, face up to it immediately and solve it. Small, inexpensive problems can become large, costly problems—fast.

8. Negotiate. Get comfortable making an offer that is to your advantage.

9. Always have an alternative handy.

10. Find out what your clients really want, not what they say that they want.

SAM'S 20 FAVORITE LAWYER TIPS

1. Always take an option when offered.

2. Read the fine print before signing.

3. Preparation beats perspiration.

4. The answer to every question begins with, "It depends..."

5. Two lawyers; three opinions.

6. If the client wins, s/he will think it was deserved. If the client loses, s/he will think it was your fault. So always get you fee in advance.

7. If it isn't in writing, it doesn't exist.

8. An oral contract is worth the paper it was written on.

9. A great way to save money on lawyers is to do the research yourself first. Find a sample contract or template and write the first draft. It costs much less to have a lawyer review and comment on a document than to prepare a document.

10. Do not start a fight where the cost of litigation will exceed the amount in controversy.

11. There is nothing more expensive than arguing over principle.

12. Go into partnership only with someone you both like and have absolute trust in.

13. Never give an option without getting something for it.

14. Never represent yourself or a close relative.

15. Never authorize or pay for work or perform work without getting a contract signed first. See #5 and #6.

16. Never discuss strategy at a restaurant, a movie theater, a cocktail party, or a public restroom.

17. Never ask a witness a question you don't know the answer to.

18. Never lend money to friends or relatives. Either say no or say it is a gift.

19. The larger the lawyer's reputation, the greater the vulnerability to being tripped up by hubris.

20. Lastly, never assume anything.

4 EXPERT WITNESS INSIDER TIPS

1. Only answer the question, as asked. "Over-answering," answering questions that aren't asked, and being too "smart" with your answers, could create problems for your client.

2. Be prepared to answer any question from opposing counsel, even if it is outside your area of expertise as defined by the pre-trial qualification disclosure. After you are asked a question on a new subject area by the other side, you are now permitted to answer any questions on that area throughout the remainder of the trial asked by your side.

3. When the opposing counsel tries to disqualify you as an expert witness, he or she needs to have a very compelling argument, or risks creating sympathy from the jury for you.

4. You have a smart opposing counsel if he or she interjects that your qualifications have already been stipulated, rather than allow your qualifications to be shared with the jury.

QUOTES FOR SUCCESS IN BUSINESS

"Success is the sum of small efforts, repeated day in and day out."

—Robert Collier

"The only place where success comes before work is in the dictionary."

—Vince Lombardi

"You don't have to be great to start, but you have to start to be great."

—Zig Ziglar

"It always seems impossible until it is done."

—Nelson Mandela

"By failing to prepare, you are preparing to fail."

—Benjamin Franklin

"Expect the best, plan for the worst, and prepare to be surprised."

—Denis Waitley

When asked how he made his living in the stock market: "I never attempted to buy at the bottom or sell at the top."

—William Krelitz, Sam's grandfather

"Give a man a fish and you feed him for a day; teach a man to fish you and feed him for a lifetime."

—*Maimonides*

"It is not so hard to earn money as to spend it well."

—*Spurgeon*

"You can't shake hands with a clenched fist."

—*Indira Ghandi*

"Giving up doesn't mean you are weak. Sometimes, it means you are strong enough and smart enough to let go and move on."

—*Oprah Winfrey*

"An investment in knowledge always pays the best interest."

—*Benjamin Franklin*

"One man pretends to be rich, yet has nothing; another pretends to be poor, yet has great wealth."

—*Proverbs 13:7-8*

"It is not enough to reach for the brass ring. You must also enjoy the merry go round."

—*Julie Andrews*

"There are but two ways of paying debt: increase of industry in raising income, increase of thrift in laying out."

—*Thomas Carlyle*

"Creditors have better memories than debtors."
—Benjamin Franklin

"Be diligent to know the state of your flocks, and attend to your herds; for riches are not forever, nor does a crown endure to all generations."
—Proverbs 27:23

"It requires a great deal of boldness and a great deal of caution to make a great fortune, and when you have it, it requires ten times as much wit to keep it."
—Ralph Waldo Emerson

"Money was never a big motivation for me, except as a way to keep score. The real excitement is playing the game."
—Donald Trump

"If you would be wealthy, think of saving as well as getting."
—Benjamin Franklin

"If money be not thy servant, it will be thy master."
—Francis Bacon

"Business is like a wheel barrow. Nothing happens until you start pushing."
—Robert Kiyosaki

"When you take risks, you learn that there will be times when you succeed and there will be times when you fail, and both are equally important."

—*Ellen DeGeneres*

"A wise man thinks ahead; a fool doesn't, and even brags about it!"

—*Proverbs 13:19*

"Buy land. They ain't making any more of the stuff."

—*Will Rogers*

"The only difference between a rich person and poor person is how they use their time."

—*Robert Kiyosaki*

"If we command our wealth, we shall be rich and free. If our wealth commands us, we are poor indeed."

—*Edmund Burke*

"A man's treatment of money is the most decisive test of his character—how he makes it and how he spends it."

—*James Moffatt*

"Save a part of your income and begin now, for the man with a surplus controls circumstances and the man without a surplus is controlled by circumstances."

—*Henry H. Buckley*

"If you do what you've always done, you'll get what you've always gotten."

—Tony Robbins

"Keep away from people who belittle your ambitions. Small people always do that, but the really great make you feel that you, too, can become great."

—Robert Kiyosaki

"If you're going to be thinking anything, you might as well think big."

—Donald Trump

"Often the difference between a successful man and a failure is not one's better abilities or ideas, but the courage that one has to bet on his ideas, to take a calculated risk, and to act."

—Maxwell Maltz

"A penny saved is better than a penny earned—because it is not taxed."

—Sam Freshman

"Annual income twenty pounds, annual expenditure nineteen six, result happiness. Annual income twenty pounds, annual expenditure twenty pounds ought and six, result misery."

—from David Copperfield by Charles Dickens

"If you give someone a fish, you have fed them for a day. But if you teach someone to fish, you have fed them for the rest of their lives."

—Old Proverb

CONCLUSION

Whether you are interested in learning more about business, real estate, syndication, or want to live a more fulfilling life, these ideas should be helpful in your life.

Always remember to be open to learning new ways to do things. That is one of the secrets to my success. I have vowed to never be old enough to know better. As soon as you think you know everything, you are doomed.

What is more important to you than acquiring success, fame, or material desires? That is real success.

I found an article in the *Jewish Journal* several years ago entitled, "The Answer is Love." It is an excerpt from *More Money Than God: Living a Rich Life Without Losing Your Soul,* by Steven Z. Leder. In it, Leder recounts being called to the bedside of an extremely famous and wealthy movie director. The elderly gentleman struggled to ask in a whisper, "What is it all for?" Searching for an answer, the Rabbi glanced at an old photograph tacked on the wall—a picture of a young couple holding hands on a park bench. "It's to love and be loved," he responded. "They understood that." The gentleman agreed.

No one's last words were "I wish I had spent more time at the office." May this book help you balance your personal and business life, and focus on what is really important to you.

ABOUT THE AUTHOR

Sam Freshman is an expert in real estate syndication and has been a partner in over 100 real estate syndications. He founded and has been chairman of Standard Management Company for over 50 years. Standard manages hundreds of millions of dollars in assets. A Stanford University and Stanford Law School graduate, Sam is Chairman Emeritus of Stanford Professionals in Real Estate (SPIRE). He has been adjunct professor of real estate law at the University of Southern California Graduate School of Business and has lectured on real estate law and syndication at the law schools of Pepperdine University, Stanford University, Loyola, University of Southern California, and University of California Los Angeles.

Sam has been a member of the American College of Forensic Examiners since 1994, and has served as an expert witness in 100 legal cases involving real estate and banking matters in both state and federal courts.

Throughout his legal and business career, Sam has provided hundreds of hours of consulting, mentoring, and workshops to help people of all ages and incomes achieve success in their lives and their businesses.

INDEX

INDEX

MORE BOOKS BY SAM FRESHMAN

Principles of Real Estate Syndication (3rd Ed.)

***TheSmartestWay™* to Save,
Why You Can't Hang on to Money
and What to Do About It**
(with Heidi Clingen)

***TheSmartestWay™* to Save More,
Making the Most of Your Money**
(with Heidi Clingen)

***TheSmartestWay™* to Save Big,
The Large Things in Life for Less**
(with Heidi Clingen)

SAMUEL K. FRESHMAN
Chairman and President
Standard Management Company
SFreshman@StandardManagement.com
(310) 410-2300

www.StandardManagement.com
www.syndicationideas.com
www.TheSmartestWay.com
www.SamuelKFreshman.com
http://bit.ly/SamFreshmanSpire

Made in the USA
San Bernardino, CA
13 April 2018